Made for
Each Other

Made for
Each Other

DEVOTIONS
for Newly Married Couples

ROY G. GESCH

CONCORDIA PUBLISHING HOUSE · SAINT LOUIS

Copyright © 1987 Concordia Publishing House
3558 S. Jefferson Avenue, St. Louis, MO 63118-3968
Manufactured in the United States of America.

Library of Congress Cataloging in Publication Data

Gesch, Roy G.
    Made for each other.
    1. Married people—Prayer-books and devotions—English. I. Title.
    BV4529.2.G47   1986   242'.64   86-17596
    ISBN 0-570-04453-7

To Dorothy,
through whom God has brought
about so much joy
and blessing throughout
our years together.

CONTENTS

PREFACE

A number of years ago, at a time when I was heavily involved in marriage counseling, I felt a tremendous need for more devotional material designed to help strengthen the marital ties. To help meet that need, my wife and I developed two small books on the essence and concerns of marriage. Though the one was geared to a husband's perspectives, the other to a wife's, they followed the same table of contents. It was our hope that they would be used privately first, then shared to open the door to further discussion and exploration.

Concordia Publishing House published these companion books under the titles *A Husband Prays* and *A Wife Prays*. Both authors and publisher have been gratified at the response.

Recently it was suggested that we take a fresh look at marriage, in the light of today's environment. Concordia published this manuscript also, *To Love and to Cherish,* and suggested a companion volume of devotions to strengthen young Christian couples as they venture forward to make a life together. That is the purpose of this book.

We pray God that it may meet and serve that purpose.

I.
THE
ESSENCE
OF
MARRIAGE

MADE FOR EACH OTHER

*S*troll along any popular beach on a hot and sultry day. The sands are overlaid with wall-to-wall bodies. Each wave of the incessant surf stands poised to deposit more human flotsam at the water's edge.

People! Masses of people! Of all shapes and sizes. Of all races and nationalities. Scanty bathing attire has become the great equalizer. It's almost impossible to distinguish rich from poor, people of high position from those of lower estate. They're just thousands and thousands of people.

Yet the little child, half-empty pop bottle in hand, threads his way between the bodies to those two who are his own special people. There are many men all around who are stronger than his father, and many women prettier than his mother. But these are his! He recognizes, knows, and loves them. No others in the surrounding thousands could ever take their place.

Multiply this scene by a million, and you appreciate the marvelous phenomenon of human relationships. Billions of people all over the earth. But here we stand, hand in hand, uniquely alone, yet together.

By God's good grace, we found each other. We hold to each other. And we are confident that God will enable us to weather all the storms through our entire life together too.

Isn't that what God had in mind in the very beginning?

> Then the Lord God said, "It is not good that the man should be alone; I will make him a helper fit for him."
> Gen. 2:18 RSV

And here we are now! By God's creating love two people, yet uniquely one. Two people, made for each other! It is indeed good!

PRAYER

*L*ord God, we thank You for each other. We see you as the wise and loving Designer and Giver of life and living relationships. We appreciate the many close friends and companions You have given us. We are fully aware of the host of the world's "beautiful people" that television and the rest of the media parade before us. But in contrast to them all, we are grateful that You brought us together. You truly made us for each other. Now we ask You to enrich our togetherness each day.

Keep us truly one in every way, that we never lose our sense of wonder over our special love for each other—or of Your special love that made us what we are. In Jesus Christ our Lord. Amen.

ESSENTIALLY YOURS

*S*incerely yours" is our customary and formal way of closing a letter. Depending on its nature, we may vary it with "Gratefully yours" or, if we feel particularly close, "Cordially," "Affectionately," or even "Lovingly yours."

In marriage we had better stick with "All my love" or "Hugs and kisses." Something to express that special closeness. Try something like "Essentially yours," and you lose a lot of points.

Yet that phrase could highlight another of the marvels of marriage. The first chapters of the Bible not only state that God chose to make a life companion *for* the other, but He also proceeded to make the one *of* the other. Unlike all else around them , these two were of the same essence. They were *essentially* the same. And they knew it.

When man first saw woman, he described her quite poetically:

> This is now bone of my bones and flesh of my flesh;
> she shall be called 'woman,' for she was taken out of
> man.
>
> Gen. 2:23

In their daily walk and talk with God, they came to know that this new life was created by God right out of man's own life. They knew from the start that the life they shared was in essence different from all other forms of life in the beautiful scene around them. They were *essentially* one. Only they!

Thank God, so are we! The life and love we share in marriage we share with no one else in quite that way. The intimacies we share go with our private territory. They are part of the essence of our marriage. They are "essentially ours."

PRAYER

*H*eavenly Father, in a day when the scientific approach is applied to everything, make us more appreciative of the simple and beautiful way Scripture describes our beginnings. We see love, wisdom, and power behind the story of creation. We see our lives in terms of goals planned by You, not as accidents caused by freak circumstances. We see mankind on a level of dignity and worth. We see ourselves moved by love and appreciation, not by animal behavior. We are grateful!

Help us appreciate also the mystery of how You brought one human life out of the other. To appreciate how uniquely one we are with each other. Help us build on this oneness, respecting, cherishing, and loving each other to the fullest. Help us do it in such a way that it truly reflects our love and respect for You too, Lord. Amen.

A GOOD CHRISTIAN MARRIAGE

What does it take to make a good Christian marriage?

Let's see! We could begin by listing love, faith, considerateness, patience, understanding.

But wait a moment! Isn't there something even more basic?

To start with the absolutely basic ingredients, we must say that it takes, first and foremost, two good Christians to make a good Christian marriage.

It takes not one but two people who are truly spiritually alive—two who are alive in Christ—two who have and share that life in the Lord Jesus Christ.

That's not the same as two people who are favorably disposed to the Christian religion—two who confessionally accept that Jesus Christ is Lord and Savior—two who go to church, perhaps even together.

It takes more to make a good Christian—and a good Christian marriage.

The Epistle of James warns us: "Faith by itself, if it is not accompanied by action, is dead" (2:17).

A Christian marriage needs more than pious words and understandings. It needs to be constructed of attitudes, emotions, and actions that all indicate vibrant spiritual life.

Essentially it is a bond, a relationship, a commitment between two followers of the Lord Jesus Christ—

two who have been "born again of water and of the Spirit" (John 3:3, 5)—two who are really living the new life God has given them.

Making a Christian marriage is not difficult in that kind of a spiritually alive environment. But without it, it is impossible. Making a marriage may be possible, even without faith. Perhaps even a reasonably good one. But at its best, it will still be only a little taste of what a good Christian marriage can be.

PRAYER

O God, it looks as if we'd best get back to the drawing board. Help us recognize that the best way to assure that our marriage is right is by making sure that we are right. Help us strengthen our spiritual foundations daily through Your Word and prayer. Regenerate us. Give us a faith that converts words into meaningful attitudes and actions. Let our whole life reflect a love that is vibrantly alive for You and for each other. Make and keep us both truly alive in Christ through Your Spirit. Amen.

FORSAKING
ALL OTHERS

A t the beginning, as our Creator instituted marriage, the uniting of a man and a woman in a unique and beautiful relationship, these words were recorded: "A man will leave his father and mother and be united to his wife, and they will become one flesh" (Gen. 2:24).

Millennia later, when asked about marriage, Jesus repeated this directive (Matt. 19:5). The apostle Paul similarly shared this principle virtually word for word (Eph. 5:31).

The message is no different for us today. As two become one in marriage—united physically, emotionally, and in every other way—they soon discover that this new togetherness calls for a lot of adjusting. One aspect of this is getting used to the idea of being married, and getting used to each other.

But the other side of the coin is the change in old relationships. Essentially it means leaving them.

"A man leaves his father and mother," Jesus says. So does a woman. But it's not just a matter of physical separation. More important is the emotional detachment.

We're not children anymore, feeling a continued dependence on our parents. We are adults. We have assumed adult responsibility. We must learn to stand on our own two feet, especially as we bring into this world new lives that are totally dependent on us.

"Leave father and mother." Yes. But not love them less. In fact, as we now look on them through mature eyes, we appreciate them all the more. We can now grasp more fully what it took for them to parent us—the sacrifices they made to meet our growing needs.

Right now, when they feel the impact of our separation, is a good time to go out of our way to express our love to them. Instead of getting all turned in on ourselves, we would do well to go out of our way to thank our parents—to ease the leaving by letting them know how much they mean to us.

In recent years a prominent telecommunications company has warmed our hearts and homes with a series of TV commercials built around the theme "Reach out and touch someone." Even though we have now left father and mother, let's make sure we continue to reach out to them, and keep in touch. Not the casual touch, which may be little more than a point of contact. But the touch of open, warm, expressed love.

PRAYER

*H*eavenly Father, we thank You for our parents. As we now make our own lives in our own home, don't ever let us get too busy to express our love and thanks to them. In Jesus. Amen.

TO BE A HUSBAND

*F*or this reason a man will leave his father and mother, and be united to his wife; and the two will become one flesh" (Eph. 5:31).

This is not suggesting or justifying today's shallow thinking that places undue emphasis on sex. Yes, the sexual relationship is a key element in a good marriage. But real togetherness is much more than "bed or bored."

The togetherness should be so complete that the wife is as much a part of her husband as is his very own body. So much so that he nourishes and cherishes her, provides and cares for her, as much as he does for himself (Eph. 5:28–29).

That's quite a tall order. As a husband, I am to be as sensitive to my wife's needs and feelings as I am to my own. I am to feel her hurts as much as mine. I am to rejoice in her good fortune as if it were mine. In fact, we are to be so "one" that her good fortune is mine.

It goes beyond feelings. I am to be sensitive enough not only to care but to do something about it.

How can two become so fully one? The key is *love:* "Husbands, love your wives, just as Christ loved the church and gave himself up for her" (Eph. 5:25).

That's not the self-seeking, self-gratifying excuse for love that predominates in the romantic interlude type of marriage so common today. This is real love— the willingness to give self, even to sacrifice self if need be for the good of the other.

My love in marriage is to be so pure and perfect that none other than Jesus Christ Himself can be the pattern to follow. Christ loved the church—His people—us—so much that He gave up, He sacrificed every-thing to help us. To save us. He did for us what we could never do for ourselves.

There's the goal for us as husbands: "Each one of you must love his wife as he loves himself" (Eph. 5:33).

It's not an option. It's a *must*. It's the husband's key to a good marriage.

PRAYER

*H*eavenly Father, after thinking through what Scripture says of a husband's role, I'm terrified. How can anyone attain the perfect love that Jesus had? But I want to try! Help me to live that kind of love, even if it is imperfect and incomplete. When I fall short, forgive, and get me started again on the way of love with Jesus. Amen.

TO BE
A WIFE

W here do I as a wife fit in? What guidelines does
Scripture offer me to help uphold my end of our
life together?

"The wife must respect her husband" (Eph. 5:33).

Respect him? What about the other way around?
Shouldn't he be respecting me?

Of course. But something much deeper and heavier
than that is expected of him—to love me so much that
he would be willing to give up all, even die for me if
necessary.

If such be his role, is anything less than corre-
sponding love and respect in order? Though 1 John 4:19
speaks of our love for Jesus, the principle applies here
too: "We love because he first loved us."

How does such love and respect show itself?

> Wives, submit to your husbands as to the Lord. For
> the husband is the head of the wife as Christ is the
> head of the church, of which he is the Savior.
>   Eph. 5:22

Regrettably some criticize and condemn this directive as outmoded and chauvinist. They've put
thumbs down without really listening.

The word *submit* unfortunately has taken on over-
tones of subservience today. It is interpreted as playing
a minor role, yielding to someone else's pressures, giving in to the boss.

To draw that conclusion out of these words is to
make Christ a demanding dictator—to suggest that we

cringe and obey Him, mostly because He is God and we are not.

How far from the truth! Were He not our Lord, we would make Him our Head. No one else is our loving Savior. No one else has made such sacrifice for our eternal good. We gladly and of our own accord submit ourselves, dedicate and commit ourselves to Him and to His service.

As a wife I also choose to love and respect my husband. Why do I greet him with a kiss, prepare his favorite meals, and try to make home a peaceful haven for him? Why do I try to keep the old boy happy? Because I'm afraid of him? Because he demands it?

No, I do it because I love him. I appreciate all the ways he shows his love to me. I want to work with him in every way to make our home a little heaven on earth.

PRAYER

Lord Jesus, as a Christian I can not do for You what You did for me. I can never repay Your saving love. But I can and do love You, and I want as best I can to prove that love to You. Let that be my pattern in marriage too. Help me to show my husband how much I appreciate his love. Help us build a strong home together, a lasting marriage filled with love. Amen.

THE
BEAUTIFUL
BRIDE

*I*n the well-known guidelines for husbands and wives in Ephesians 5 there is a wonderful picture—that of a radiant and beautiful bride. Because it is a sharp departure from the practical guidelines, we sometimes pass over it too quickly. That's unfortunate.

The bride is wearing the prettiest (and costliest) dress she's ever worn. It's pure white, no spots or wrinkles. She's taken great care with her makeup and hair too.

The groom is proud of her as she walks down the aisle. As he glances over the assembly, he is happy the relatives and friends see her just as he does—radiantly beautiful.

He has anxiously awaited this moment when they two might become one. Others had pointed out that there could be problems, that she had faults and failings, and that they did not regard her as beautiful as he did.

But that did not cause him to back off. Background and shortcomings were of lesser importance. What mattered more than anything else was that he truly loved her.

> Husbands, love your wives, just as Christ loved the church and gave himself up for her to make her holy, cleansing her by the washing with water through the word, and to present her to himself as a radiant church, without stain or wrinkle or any other blemish, but holy and blameless.
>
> Eph. 5:25–27

What a beautiful picture of the love and oneness between Christ and His church! What a perfect pattern for husband and wife!

Christ chose an imperfect bride. We, who by faith are united with him, are imperfect people. But He loved us anyway.

He didn't turn away, criticize, or demand that we conceal our imperfections. In His all-encompassing love He chose to deal with our faults and imperfections another way. He made our debts His and paid for them. He took our spots and wrinkles, and gave us a new and clean beginning.

Because of His love, we are His partners in a marriage made in heaven. We don't have to feel guilty or inadequate because of our sinfulness or frailty.

We are forgiven! We are beautiful! For we are loved!

PRAYER

"Jesus, Your blood and righteousness
My beauty are, my glorious dress."

Thank You for covering our imperfections with Your perfect love. We know that now, by Your grace, we can stand unashamed—even before our heavenly Father, our eternal Judge. Help us to accept and love each other just as we are—the way You love us. Amen.

UNFADING BEAUTY

There is another chapter in the Bible that gives helpful and enriching directives to husbands and wives. In this case the words come from the pen of the apostle Peter:

> Wives, ... be submissive to your husbands so that, if any of them do not believe the word, they may be won over without talk by the behavior of their wives, when they see the purity and reverence of your lives.
> 1 Peter 3:1–2

Once again we must remember that the word "submissive" does not imply either subservience or lower status. It the natural response of love to love—as we submit ourselves in love to our Lord Jesus Christ, who in love gave His all for us.

One of the hopes and goals in marriage is to achieve a perfect oneness. That includes the joy of sharing our faith, of being one in Christ.

Peter says that goal can be realistic, even if one does not yet believe the Word. A wife can win her husband over to Christ. (Of course, a husband can similarly win his wife for Christ.) But the power of a good Christian example is far more effective in this than any amount of talking and preaching.

Peter pursues this further, by commenting on wives' true beauty: "Your beauty should not come from outward adornment, such as braided hair and the wearing of gold jewelry and fine clothes. Instead, it should be that of your inner self, the unfading beauty of a gentle and quiet spirit, which is of great worth in God's sight" (1 Peter 3:3–4).

Despite what they say, clothes do not make the

man—or the woman either. Hairstyles, cosmetics, jewelry, and clothes can enhance a woman's beauty, but the beauty is innate in her. It's more than physical appearance, though that is part of it. It is the whole person—body, mind, and spirit.

That kind of winsome inner beauty Peter calls "unfading beauty."

He says it is "of great worth in God's sight." But it certainly is also in her husband's sight. He has the chance to observe and appreciate her most of all.

And what does this all mean to the husband? "Husbands, in the same way be considerate as you live with your wives, and treat them with respect . . . as heirs with you of the gracious gift of life" (1 Peter 3:7).

What a beautiful picture of a marriage that is really united and blessed by love! One in love now—and heirs together of unending life and love!

PRAYER

*L*ord God, give us such unfading beauty and worth, that we may be heirs together "of the gracious gift of life," the gift purchased and won for us by our Lord Jesus Christ. Amen.

LIFETIME WARRANTY

*I*t feels so good to invest our hard-earned money in a product that has a lifetime warranty.

In a junkyard world of broken and obsolescent wares, here at last is something that should stand up under use, and still be functional after all the installments have been paid.

A lifetime warranty. But wait a minute! What does that mean? Whose lifetime? Mine? Yours?

It's a bit deflating to learn that it really has nothing to do with our lifetime. Usually it is the lifetime of the product. The company will stand behind it for what it considers a normal period of use. Or as long as it still has replacement parts for that since-outmoded product. Or as long as the company remains solvent.

A lifetime warranty. But is it?

At the altar we made a lifetime promise to each other, and anticipated a lifetime warranty. We saw marriage as a lifetime commitment. We looked forward to a lifetime of joy and blessing.

But what about that promise and warranty? In today's context what does "lifetime" mean? Our lifetime? The lifetime of the marriage? Or the readiness of the present company to stand behind it?

Apparently many today have forgotten the wording of the promise. Or have taken it lightly. What we said—and, we hope, meant—was "Till death do us part." "I pledge my faithfulness to you as long as God gives us life."

In Ecclesiastes 9:9 we find these words: "Enjoy life

with your wife, whom you love, all the days of this . . . life that God has given you."

That's all we want, and all we expect! Lord, make it so! Make and keep us truly one all the days of this life that You have given us.

PRAYER

*F*aithful God, You never go back on Your Word. We can bank on every promise You ever made. We lay claim to heaven and unending life even now because Jesus, in accord with Your promise, has gained and given it to us.

Now help us to be true to our word too—especially to the promise and commitment we made to each other in marriage. Help us to find the full lifetime of joy and blessing that You intended for us from the very beginning. In Jesus' name we ask it. Amen.

WHAT GOD HAS JOINED TOGETHER . . .

When Jesus stated the basic premise of marriage, He said: "They are no longer two, but one. Therefore what God has joined together, let man not separate" (Matt. 19:6).

We have a unique bond and commitment in our marriage. It's totally different from other legal agreements, business contracts, or informal personal pacts.

All of these are intended to be binding. Some even attach heavy penalties if the agreement is broken. But only of the marriage promise and union can it be said that it is sealed and blessed by God Himself. "God has joined us together."

There's something strangely twisted when a man or woman will make any sacrifice to keep a business deal, yet take a casual attitude toward the marriage promise.

The Lord who joined us in marriage looks at it differently. "What God has joined together, let not man separate."

"To the married I give this command (not I, but the Lord): A wife must not separate from her husband. . . . And a husband must not divorce his wife" (1 Cor. 7:10–11).

"But let's be practical," many around us say. "That's great for people who hit it off well. But what about the other half of the population that is disappointed in their marriages? Do you think God expects them to be miserable all the rest of their lives? A good legal divorce could better the situation all the way around. After all, even the Bible says there are just causes for divorce."

That's true, the Bible does say a person is no longer bound to a spouse who is unfaithful in marriage—who has broken the vow of love by adultery or unchastity. Yet when church leaders asked Jesus if divorce was not a permissible option, He replied, "Moses permitted you to divorce your wives because your hearts were hard. But it was not this way from the beginning" (Matt. 19:8).

That's not the way God intended or made marriage.

Divorce may be understandable where a person has never opened his or her heart to the love or will of God. There's not much real fiber or fabric to hold that kind of home together.

But we are Christ's people. That's a whole different story. We have a different goal, a different pattern, a different motivation—plus God's blessing. Lord, we want to work at making a good marriage—not look for a way out.

PRAYER

Father, we would rededicate ourselves to a strong and lasting marriage. You joined us in our marriage. Provide us now with Your constant blessing, though our Lord Jesus Christ. Amen.

IT'S DECISION-MAKING TIME!

*T*he art of making decisions, especially good ones, is not easy.

It can even be a bit scary at times.

The decision that brought us together as husband and wife was certainly not easy. Oh, we loved each other all right, and we truly did want to spend our lives together. But to actually make that decision and commitment was still a bit difficult.

It was so final. It meant: "This is it! No more playing the field! No more independent thinking or planning. No more giving in to my every little whim or desire. This is real, and it is for keeps!"

But we made the decision, and we are grateful we did. Our fears were unfounded. What we gave up was supplanted with joys and blessings far greater than those we had. God was truly good to us in bringing us to this oneness.

We did it and we're glad! That's the way with all good decisions. We never look back on them with regret.

But yesterday's good decisions do not necessarily make tomorrow's easier. Like the decision, which runs such a beautiful parallel to our marriage promise—the decision to make a full commitment to our God.

God's people have been challenged to make that decision in every age. One of the most dramatic is recorded in Joshua 24. The people had finally reached and settled in the Promised Land. Now Joshua challenges them all to make a pact of loyalty to God: "Honor the Lord and serve Him sincerely and faithfully. . . . If you are not willing to serve Him, decide today whom you will serve. . . . As for my family and me, we will serve the Lord."

Their response was beautiful. They did make a decision, and it was a good one: "God brought our fathers and us out of slavery . . . we saw the miracles that He performed. He kept us safe wherever we went. . . . So we also will serve the Lord; He is our God" (Joshua 24:14–18 TEV).

That kind of a good decision, coupled with the good decision that established our marriage, lays strong foundations under our home. Such strength does not come by itself. It requires both the readiness to make those decisions and the determination to follow through on them both.

PRAYER

G racious Father, You know the moments of hesitation that preceded our decision to become one. You also know the temptations that dilute our faith. But we made our decisions to stand firm and faithful, to each other and to You. Strengthen us daily through Your Word, so that we can live by these decisions and keep our promises holy and unbroken until death. In Jesus. Amen.

II.
MARRIAGE
ENRICH-
MENT

"GO FOR
THE GOLD!"

There's a tongue-in-cheek story that circulated after the Olympic Games. It told of an Olympic athlete who proved he was the best by winning the gold medal in his event. He was so excited that he took it home and bronzed it!

"Go for the gold!" That phrase became a common byline. And a good one it is!

It's hard to imagine a trainee whose competitive ambition was to strive to be number 12, or even to come in second or third. The gold medal, coming in first, was the ultimate dream.

Yet, win a medal or not, all competitors had this deep and lasting satisfaction. They gave it their best shot. Every one of them was in that select group set apart from the rest of the world, a small group who had worked hard to be the best they could be.

That's a good goal for our personal lives too, and for our married lives. "Go for the gold!"

Our life together may not be perfect. There may be others around us who may seem to be more fulfilled and enriched in many ways. But they may be thinking the same about us and our marriage.

What matters most is that we strive together to be the best we can be. It's not for a medal, a ribbon, or a crown. These eventually become memento clutter. It's what we gain and what we become personally that really matters.

Paul encouraged his Christian friends:

> Run in such a way as to get the prize. Everyone

who competes in the games goes into strict training.
They do it to get a crown that will not last; but we
do it to get a crown that will last forever.

1 Cor. 9:24–25

There are blessings and prizes that never lose their
worth or glory. They are not earned. God gives them
to those who prevail. We will find them in our personal
life, in our marriage, and in our spiritual life together,
as we "go for the gold."

That's the ultimate goal. We dare not dream or
pray or work for anything less.

PRAYER

L ord Jesus, set our sights high. Give us the drive
to put everything into our marriage to make it the
best it can possibly be. Don't let us settle for lesser
goals, or bronze over the gold we have already been
given. Make us "faithful unto death" that we together
may receive Your promised "crown of life." Amen.

TIME FLIES WHEN YOU'RE IN LOVE!

*J*acob served seven years to get Rachel, but they seemed like only a few days to him because of his love for her" (Gen. 29:20).

How beautiful! Jacob and Rachel—young people so much in love with each other that they were willing to put up with the unjust demands and despicable deceit of her father just to be together!

Rather than defy him, they worked hard and patiently over many years to start their marriage on a solid footing. All the while they could only dream and anticipate.

How could they possibly endure the unbearable? There's really only one answer. Theirs was so great a love that those long and arduous years "seemed like only a few days."

It's wonderful what love can do. Paul reminded his Christian friends in 1 Corinthians 13:7, "[Love] always protects, always trusts, always hopes, always perseveres."

Love is able to make us bear and endure all things.

It's true! Wonderfully true!

How often has our love helped us over the rough spots, even before marriage, and certainly much more in these present years?

Neither love nor marriage can immunize us against problems or sorrows. Dark clouds cast shadows over even the happiest of homes.

But they pass. When they do, real joy is ours when we can recognize that, more than anything else, it was our love for each other, and God's love for us, that carried us through.

It made our time of struggle seem but a few days now that we look back on it.

PRAYER

*L*ord Jesus, there's so much we would like to ask You. About Your love—Your willingness to come to us, to live with us, to die for us—Your readiness to sacrifice all to win an eternal victory for us. Lord, how could love ever be that strong? As You look back on those years of hard service, do You feel it was worth it? Are we worth it? Do those years now seem to You but a few days because of the love You have for us?

Lord Jesus, we thank You for that love. Now can You give us such love too? Will you, Lord? Amen! Let it be so!

LET LOVE
BE GENUINE

*I*t's interesting to note how various translators and editors have expressed this important directive in Romans 12:9.

"Let love be genuine" (RSV).

"Love must be completely sincere" (TEV).

In contrast to these positive approaches, several highlight the truth by coming at it from the opposite direction.

"Let us have no imitation Christian love" (Phillips).

"Do not let your love be a pretense" (Jerusalem Bible).

"Don't just pretend that you love others: really love them" (The Living Bible).

The original Greek manuscripts use the word *non-hypocritical*. The picture is of the stage actor who wore the mask to convey the moods and feelings of the play. It hid the real person underneath. The audience saw only what the actor wanted it to see.

All of life is complicated by the practice of mask-wearing. It is common in business, in international relations, in society in general. Sometimes what is deemed to be tact and diplomacy is nothing more than the art of disguise. But when the pretense is discovered, the trust which must underlie all human relationships is lost.

Such game-playing can be damaging in all of life. But the setting in which pretense is most devastating is marriage.

Our marriage is built on trust. We have, and we must ever have, complete confidence in each other. Not just confidence that we are both good people, or that we are good for each other. The bedrock undergirding our marriage is that we truly love each other. Love is the heart of our marriage.

There is no "reasonably accurate facsimile" that can be substituted for love. Either we love, or we don't. All the game-playing in the world can't make a marriage live when it has become apparent that love is not genuine or sincere.

The apostle John, who was noted for his love, counsels: "My children, our love is not to be just words or mere talk, but something real and active" (1 John 3:18 Jerusalem Bible).

O God, keep our love like that!

PRAYER

L ord Jesus, we know that love is not something that can be turned on or off at will. Nor can it be faked. It's how we feel about each other. We confess that our love—for each other and for You—seems very shallow compared with the love You have for us. So we pray that You will move us by Your love to seek and find a deeper and richer love. Don't ever let us make the mistake of pretending to love. If there are days when it seems harder to love, help us to work it out together. Amen.

WHAT DOES IT TAKE?

Occasionally before marriage, a couple gets cold feet. Are we really ready? Do we really have what it takes to make a good and lasting marriage?

We usually dispel our doubts by focussing on one word—LOVE. We enjoy being together. We want to make a life together, because we love each other. Surely, everything will be all right!

If we had had to define what we mean by "love," we might never have taken the step. But because love is recognized more by the ways it expresses itself, we felt we were ready.

Look at this catalog of character traits: "Love, joy, peace, patience, kindness, goodness, faithfulness, gentleness, self-control."

Don't they describe well what it takes to make a good marriage?

When things go wrong between us, it's because one of us—or both of us—have let down in several of these areas. Can we really be that perfect kind of person? What's the secret?

That catalog of virtues was lifted right out of Paul's letter to the Galatians. The whole verse reads, "The fruit of the Spirit is love, joy, peace, patience, kindness, goodness, faithfulness, gentleness and self-control" (Gal. 5:22–23).

What is suggested is that we don't become good husbands and wives by reading marriage manuals or lying on a psychiatrist's couch. Being a good spouse lies in the same territory as being a good Christian.

The qualities we look for in each other are labeled "the fruit of the Spirit." Paul calls this "living by the Spirit," and "keeping in step with the Spirit" (5:25). It is a whole new nature and way of life for "those who belong to Christ Jesus" (5:24).

This is what the Holy Spirit implants and works in us who, by His grace, are alive in Christ. We can't take credit. This is a change God makes in us as we strive to keep in step with Him.

The virtues that make for a good marriage are not just good manners that can be put on or off like a clean shirt or blouse, changed for the occasion. They become our God-molded character, our whole being. And at the center of it all is love.

"Over all these virtues put on love, which binds all together in perfect unity" (Col. 3:14).

PRAYER

*H*oly Spirit, thank You! Through the Word, You brought us to a living faith in Christ. Keep this faith alive, by Your Word, so that we may bear this much-needed "fruit"—to enrich our marriage, and prove Your goodness to the whole world. Amen.

LET THE LIGHT SHINE!

good marriage, like all the rest of life, is totally

A good marriage, like all the rest of life, is totally affected by these words of Scripture in Ephesians 5:8: "You were once darkness, but now you are light in the Lord."

There's really no middle ground between light and darkness. Our way of life will be representative of one or the other.

A few verses earlier St. Paul reminded the Ephesian Christians of some of the things that were typical of the "darkness" with which they were surrounded— "sexual immorality, impurity, greed."

The mythological goddess Diana set the tone of the city in which they lived. Prostitution, heterosexual and homosexual, played a big part in their celebrations. Christians had a rough time of it in that setting. They were ridiculed and hated as prudes and puritans.

Yet God constantly reminded: Such things as they saw daily all around them "are improper for God's holy people" (5:3). "Have nothing to do with the fruitless deeds of darkness, but rather expose them" (5:11).

Let them be seen for what they really are.

That's the challenge that faces us today too. Groups of people with alternate lifestyles are militantly "coming out of the closet." They no longer choose to hide what they are or what they do. They're encouraging one another by strength of numbers. Yet the fact still remains, "It is shameful even to mention what the disobedient do in secret" (5:12).

It's bad enough to talk about it, much more to flaunt it openly. "God's wrath comes on those who are disobedient. Therefore do not be partners with them" (5:6–7).

In or out of the closet, God's judgment remains the same.

The lines are clearly distinguishable. There's light and there's darkness. There are those obedient to God and those disobedient.

As those who are "light in the Lord," we have a firm directive, "Live as children of light" (5:8). We can not compromise our convictions and principles.

Infidelities and indiscretions, secret faults and pet sins cast shadows of darkness on life and marriage. They set the stage for distrust and erode the foundations of love.

God help us to see them for what they are, and to protect our home from such damaging shadows.

PRAYER

*L*ord Jesus, You brought new light and life to this world. Let us never again be content to frequent the neighborhood of darkness and death. Help us to live truly as children of light. Amen.

WHAT WOULD YOU HAVE ME DO?

*I*t's exciting when someone breaks out of a shell!

It is so easy to get turned in on ourselves. Self-conscious, self-loving, self-seeking, self-serving comes so naturally.

Comfortable though self-centeredness may be, it is a form of imprisonment. It's difficult to break out of such confining attitudes and habits.

It's also difficult to have a good marriage in that kind of situation. And hard to be a good Christian, when we're more in love with ourselves than with our good and gracious God.

The blueprint laid out for our lives calls for a complete turnabout: Christ "died for all, that those who live should no longer live for themselves but for him who died for them and was raised again" (2 Cor. 5:15).

Paul, the greatest missionary the world has ever seen, experienced that turnabout dramatically. He had set a willful course of prejudice and blazed a trail of hatred, fighting Christ all the way. But once he had met Jesus, the first thing he did was ask: "Lord, what [wilt thou] have me to do?" (Acts 9:6 KJV). He became a totally changed man.

What a glorious new dimension our lives take on when we begin to ask that same question. In the morning as we awaken, "Lord, what would You have us do today?" At the breakfast or dinner table, in our time of family devotions, "Lord, what would You have us do?"

As we tackle our daily responsibilities, "Lord, what would You have us do?"

It's no longer "Me first, others next, God last." Now the progression is "God first, others next, me last."

What's interesting is that we soon discover we're not left holding an empty bag. In fact, we end up more blessed than ever before.

For we become more aware of how God has been putting us first all along. And we experience a wonderfully deeper bond as husband and wife, as we now approach each other with the same question, "Dear, what can I do for you?"

PRAYER

*J*esus, we can not question Your love for us. You came to serve, not to be served. You proved Your infinite love throughout Your life, but most of all as You died for us. Turn us around, so that our thoughts and acts will also prove love—our love for You, and for each other. Amen.

THE SCHEME OF LIFE

When you think about it—which we seldom do—there's something beautiful about the matter-of-fact way the first human birth is recorded: "Adam lay with his wife Eve, and she became pregnant and gave birth to Cain. She said, 'With the help of the Lord I have brought forth a man'" (Gen. 4:1).

This first birth record also contains the first reference to sexual intercourse. And all of this is linked together with giving praise and thanks to God. It should be that way. Right?

We are attuned to thanking God for the gift of a healthy child.

In church as well as at home we also express gratitude that the months of anxious waiting and the hours of pain are over.

But the way the media and modern mind exploit sex, we feel a bit uncomfortable with the idea of thanking God for sex itself.

It was not like that in the Garden of Eden. Adam and Eve were perfectly at ease in their nakedness in each other's presence. But once Satan had succeeded in tempting them away from God's perfect ways, they became embarrassed.

We can't turn the clock back. Our world today is a far cry from what our Creator originally designed. The stains of sin sully human life. But that shouldn't prevent us from recognizing how wonderfully God made us, and from appreciating sex as a beautiful part of that creation.

What could be more perfect than how God made man and woman different from each other, yet complementary to each other? Every organ in the reproductive system is uniquely designed to enable the whole life cycle to function with precision. And all this is enhanced with strong, pleasurable drives and feelings.

Unfortunately, man has devised ways to spoil and pervert sex, and use it as a cheap tool for self-gratification. But that shouldn't deprive us Christians of the wonder and enjoyment of the sexual privilege in marriage.

Sexual attraction played its part in bringing us together. The intimacy in our relationship sets it a level above all others. The pleasure of holding each other in our arms rivals the joy of cradling a newborn child in those arms.

It's all so beautiful and wonderful! We should thank God continually for making it so!

PRAYER

*F*ather, thank You for making us wholly and intimately one. Our moments of private closeness are special gifts of Your love. Shield us from all temptations that might destroy the fulfillment we find completely in each other. Amen.

YOU ARE WHAT YOU EAT

We get tired of worn slogans like "You are what you eat." But we still need to be reminded that what we put into our bodies—and our minds—really does matter.

We have daily minimum needs of certain essential food substances. To deprive ourselves of them may mean not reaching our full potential of health or vitality.

We are not benefited by junk foods. The more junk we take in, the less likely we are to have a good appetite when nourishing foods are set before us.

So what we take in has a direct effect on what we become. That principle holds true in every area of life. "Like newborn babies, crave pure spiritual milk, so that by it you may grow up in your salvation, now that you have tasted that the Lord is good" (1 Peter 2:2).

We need to develop an appetite for not only what tastes good, but for what will do us the most good. We need to fill our lives with whatever will make us the healthiest and strongest—spiritually, mentally, and emotionally, as well as physically.

We need quality time together on activities that will enrich and nurture us. We need to put into our minds and souls vitamin-packed materials that will build up our immunities against the moral contagion around us, and prevent spiritual malnutrition.

We are fortunate that we don't have to go scouting around in a confused attempt to pinpoint what is good for us. We have already tasted and found that our Lord Jesus Christ is good, and that He already has provided us with the best that can be offered, the "pure spiritual milk" of His Word.

At home, at church—wherever we are and whatever we are doing—His ready supply is available. There's only one thing that can keep us from the growth and strength that "pure spiritual milk" can provide. We lose out only if we do not use it!

PRAYER

*D*evelop in us a craving for Your Word, most gracious God! Whet our appetite so that we will take more time together to be strengthened and nourished by that Word. By filling us with this right food, help us grow together as healthy and mature Christians— for the sake of our marriage as well as for our personal good. In the name of Jesus, who is both water and bread of life to all believers. Amen.

WHERE ARE WE GOING?

D o two walk together unless they have agreed to
do so?" (Amos 3:3).

Can two continue to walk together, unless they are
agreed on where they are going?

Imagine the confusion if one day you announced:
"Come on! Jump in the car. We're taking off on a two-
week vacation."

"Where are we going?" "Why didn't you let me know
earlier so I could have prepared?" "How can we pack
when we don't even know where we will be?"

It can be done. But there's likely to be a fair amount
of tension and disagreement before things fall into
place. A little bit of joint planning would have pre-
vented that.

Where are *we* going? In our personal lives? In our
marriage? We are no longer two people on individual
courses, hoping they will converge. We walk together
now. So where are we going?

Our lives are shared now. Our ambitions. Our
dreams. We map out our course together. Our future
is shaped by teamwork. It's like pilot and flight engi-
neer working together, each concerned with their
course and security, and each tuned in to the control
center.

If we don't take enough time to share our thoughts
and feelings, if we don't talk things out, how can we be
agreed? How can we stay on course? Such togetherness
will not last long.

It is important to agree in our walk together, and

to keep in touch with our control center together. How fortunate we are to have a God who keeps a watchful eye on us—who stands ready at all times to guide and help us in every way.

In His Word He charted the best way for us. It's always right at our fingertips. And He is always there, unless we lose contact by switching Him off.

Here again a key element is time. Time to reach agreement with each other, and time to get and stay in tune with God. But taking that time averts a lot of dead ends, detours, and undesired destinations.

Let's make and take the time every day to be sure we are really going in the right direction together, and together with God.

PRAYER

S how me your ways, O Lord, teach me your paths; guide me in your truth and teach me, for you are God my Savior." Amen.

Psalm 25:4–5

GROWTH AND MATURITY

One of the healthiest—and most beautiful—statements a husband or wife can make to the other is "I love you more than yesterday, but less than tomorrow."

Love, like every other living thing, must also grow and develop. Anything that remains static will begin to fade and deteriorate.

A maturing Christian love is an exciting form of adventure all on its own. There was no denying the excitement of our love when we first stood at the altar and made our promises to each other. But since that day we have made continuing discoveries about each other, and our appreciation of each other has grown.

The shape and scope of our love changes almost daily. Feelings once generated by impulse and attraction now are more reflective of understanding. Our home is blessed as our love goes through this process of growing and maturing.

What Paul once wrote to his Christian friends in Thessalonica applies in double force to marriage: "May the Lord make your love increase and overflow for each other" (1 Thess. 3:12).

Increase—ever growing. *Overflow*—no limits. What a meaningful prayer! What a blessing when two people experience the answer to that prayer!

It's interesting to note how, as love matures, we become less concerned about self, and more concerned about each other: "When I was a child, I talked like a child, I thought like a child, I reasoned like a child. When I became a man, I put childish ways behind me" (1 Cor. 13:11).

Thank God, we grow out of our obsession to have our own way—our pickiness and intolerance in petty differences and disagreements—our tendencies to manipulate by bullying or nagging—or to win out by pouting and the silent treatment.

Thank God, we grow to a point where we no longer see our life together as "the battle of the sexes"—where the object is to best each other—to gain the upper hand—to be the winner.

For in marriage such competition is a childish holdover. Such game-playing produces no winners, only losers.

PRAYER

*J*esus, we remember how You said: "A new command I give you: Love one another. As I have loved you, so you must love one another" (John 13:34). That never seemed like a new commandment. That theme runs through all of Scripture. But as we have grown and matured, it has become more apparent that its newness lies in attaining a love like Yours. Help us to increase and overflow in such unselfish love for each other. Make our marriage a training ground, so that such love may become our total way of life. Amen.

HELP US, LORD!

*H*ow often as children we made a mess of something that lay a little beyond our ability. Our parents stood quietly by, ready to step in and help. But we rejected their offer, stubbornly insisting, "I want to do it myself!" And we failed!

Some of us never grow out of the self-reliance syndrome. But the *greater* danger as we grow up is the feeling that we *must* do it ourselves.

The reasons for it vary. A perfectionist obsession that no one else can do it quite as well. A fear that someone else may take part of the credit. A complex that we don't want to feel obligated to anyone else.

So tensions are born and pressures mount. Potentially good team relationships never materialize. Exhaustion and frayed nerves set in, and perhaps even worse.

Why, when it is so unnecessary?

As Christians we should be well aware that there is much that we can not do by ourselves. God may let us share in the process of bringing a new life into this world, but only He can bring about the miracle of such new life.

We can live morally responsible lives, but only Jesus, through His sacrifice of self, was able to remove the all-too-evident stains that still label us sinners.

By faith we can lay claim to the crown of everlasting life, but it is ours only because Jesus gained it and gives it to us.

Rather do it ourselves? No way! We show faith and common sense when we take recourse in promises like Is. 41:10:

Do not fear, for I am with you;
    do not be dismayed, for I am your God;
I will strengthen you and help you;
    I will uphold you with my righteous right
        hand.

Perhaps when we've learned to seek and accept God's help on a daily basis, we will seek and accept help from others also. That's especially important at home. Marriage at its best is a partnership. The old word *help-meet* is right on target.

We don't have to fail alone when we can succeed together. In fact, we need never fail. Nor will we if God is central in our partnership.

PRAYER

Almighty God, give us such joy in Your promises that we never feel despair or the emptiness of trying to go it alone. Strengthen us, help us, uphold us. Bind us in a partnership where we know we can always depend on each other, and on You. We ask it in Jesus' name. Amen.

WE NEED
EACH OTHER

Time just does not stand still. Nor does it come in unlimited supply. One day each of us will reach the finishing line, and we will stand before our Maker face to face.

"Let us hold unswervingly to the hope we profess, for he who promised is faithful. And let us consider how we may spur one another on toward love and good deeds. Let us not give up meeting together, . . . but let us encourage one another—and all the more as you see the Day approaching" (Heb. 10:23–25).

That's nothing to be afraid of—not for us Christians. But that realization should make us all think seriously about what we are doing with the time God is giving us now. We can fritter it away or we can grasp the opportunities God provides and make good use of them.

The verses above remind that we have a God who will never go back on His promises. When He says He is with us always, caring for us with all His love and power, He means it. When He says that through Jesus He forgives all wrong and makes eternal life a free gift for us, He means it. We can be more sure of that than of the continued existence of the planet on which we live.

How much we need to hold on to that certainty! Not just to profess that faith in the right words, but to live that faith out in our daily doings. And to hold to our God firmly enough that we are not swayed by the adverse winds that assail us daily.

It's not easy to hold unswervingly to our faith, is it? That's where we really need each other—"to spur one another on toward love and good deeds." Who can do this better than husband and wife? Who is in a better position to encourage?

This is right at the heart of a meaningful relationship. A home without it is missing a vital element. No other common interests or activities can ever be a substitute. They are more like paint or wallpaper. They're not the stuff to give strength to a home.

Public worship carries it even further. Now we are in a broader fellowship where we all are strengthening and encouraging each other. We need this too. Our fellow Christians also need the bolstering of faith that we can provide. We need each other, even as we need the Word.

Let's not neglect these opportunities to meet together—to worship together. More than we often realize, such moments are a catalyst to real togetherness.

PRAYER

*F*ather, we're impressed at how Jesus went to the synagogue to worship, "as was His custom" (Luke 4:16). The people at church didn't accept Him, or even listen to Him. But that did not stop Him. Help us to get so tuned in that we cherish and make full use of our togetherness, at home and at church. Amen.

III.
PRACTICAL
LIVING

WHO DO YOU THINK YOU ARE?

J ust who do you think you are?"

That simple question, properly asked, can certainly cut anyone down to size.

And it should! Few things can damage a marriage more—or any human relationship—than illusions of being what we are not.

An inferiority complex may prevent people from reaching their full potential, but so can a superiority complex—that feeling of being a cut above others.

As long as we feel we are "the Greatest," we will never strive to grow in greatness. And we will expect and demand more of others than we do of ourselves.

It's pretty hard to keep love alive that way.

But how do we achieve that delicate balance between thinking too little or too much of ourselves?

Part of the secret is revealed in Romans 12:16: "Live in harmony with one another. Do not be proud. . . . Do not be conceited." Jesus puts it this way (Matt. 22:39): "Love your neighbor as yourself." We must nurture the same high regard for one another—especially as husband and wife. We may not be at all alike. But neither is superior to the other. Together we make a good life and a good marriage.

There's yet another secret to popping the empty bubbles of conceit. The apostle Paul put his finger on it when he confessed in 1 Cor. 15:10: "By the grace of God I am what I am."

He didn't put himself down. He never belittled his accomplishments. But he knew where the credit belonged. By God's grace and with God's help he had become what he was, and had achieved what he had done.

That's the key element for our home too. We're two people accepted just as we are. But by God's grace and with God's help we can build and we are building a good marriage, a good life together.

Thank You, Lord!

PRAYER

*H*eavenly Father, give us the ability to see ourselves as others see us. Then give us the courage to work to become the way You would rather see us. By Your grace it can happen! In this way enrich our togetherness, and deepen our love for each other, and strengthen our home. In Jesus we ask it. Amen.

THE MIRRORED IMAGE

No matter how much we enjoyed our vacation, there comes that dreaded moment when we look at the pictures we took. That moment can do much to strain the bonds of blissful love.

"How could you?" "Why do you always snap the shutter before we are ready?" "You always make me look so awful!"

We carefully resist the temptation to say, "But dear, that is the way you look! It's the real you!"

People who are frequently photographed soon develop a consciousness for "poise"—a certain way to tilt the head, plant the feet, and place the hands. What may seem a bit artificial at first becomes force of habit.

Affectation? Not really. It's more a matter of seeing and remembering. And doing something about it. The role of the camera is identical to the role of a mirror, as is brought out in these interesting and helpful verses:

> Do not merely listen to the word, and so deceive yourselves. Do what it says. Anyone who listens to the word but does not do what it says is like a man who looks at his face in a mirror and, after looking at himself, goes away and immediately forgets what he looks like. But the man who looks intently into the perfect law that gives freedom, and continues to do this, not forgetting what he has heard, but doing it—he will be blessed in what he does.
>
> James 1:22–25

God's Word, like a mirror or camera, does a beautiful job of showing us what we are really like. Sometimes this hurts; it shatters our illusions.

Though we readily confess that we are imperfect, sinners by God's standards, we still like to think we're basically very good. As husband and wife too, we see ourselves as loving, considerate, generous, understanding, sensitive, helpful . . . Need we go on?

On a scale of 1 to 10 we surely rate pretty high, don't we?

Maybe it's time we sit down again and, using God's Word (especially the Ten Commandments) as a mirror or camera, discuss openly and lovingly what improvements might be in order.

We may get to see faults and blemishes in ourselves that our loved ones have put up with a long time. Petty irritants of which we have not even been conscious.

Then comes the moment of truth! Are we willing to change? "He who does not forget what he has heard, but does it . . . will be blessed in what he does." That's a promise!

PRAYER

*L*ord, give us the grace to grow daily, and to accept the changes that growth inevitably brings. In Jesus. Amen.

STAYING ALIVE!

A series of television commercials effectively puts the finger on an ever-present danger—monotony and dull routine. It is so easy to slip into a rut, and so hard to get out.

The commercials depict a group of workers shuffling off to lunch. Their faces are expressionless, their eyes dull. Unemotionally they drone on about "same place" and "same thing."

When it comes right down to it, what can we expect? We start and stop work at the same time every day. Our coffee and lunch breaks are regulated by the clock and boring menus. We commute on the same roads and see the same scenery. The hours pass slowly in the company of the same people.

What's more, we develop other routines at home— around bed, bath, table, couch, and TV. Sometimes we really feel trapped, screaming to get out.

Familiar paths may offer a sense of comfortable security. But they can also drain off all the excitement and adventure of life.

God never planned for us to be dead on the vine. The name of the game, as He envisioned and offers it, is "Staying Alive!"

"I am the vine," Jesus says. "You are the branches. If a man remains in me and I in him, he will bear much fruit; apart from me you can do nothing" (John 15:5).

Life's greatest adventures are ours when we wake up to what is possible when Christ lives in us, and we live in Him.

Peter, Andrew, James, and John had a comfortable life as fishermen. The way ahead, when they turned their lives over to Jesus, was difficult and dangerous. But they became involved in the excitement of a resurrection and eternal victory, and, under God's guidance and blessing, helped to turn the world rightside up.

Saul seemed happy with his books and companions in a dead church. But when Christ made a new man of him, as the apostle Paul he found joy and blessing in the challenge of spreading the good news of the Savior's love in one country after another.

If life is getting monotonous, let's break the pattern. Let's see what new challenges God is offering us, and let's muster up the courage and faith to make a few changes.

Let's stay alive—God's way!

PRAYER

*L*ord Jesus, we know You are the vine, we the branches, and that, as we remain alive in You, we can bear much fruit. We want to accomplish much that is good. We also believe that You will give us what we wish so that, as Your people, we can live life to the fullest Your way. Make our life together a daily exciting adventure—for our good and for Your glory. Amen.

WHEN WE'VE BEEN HURT

I can tolerate a lot of pain. But I can't take it when *you* hurt me, and I'm not going to let you hurt me anymore!"

Sounds familiar. So does "I'll get even with you if it's the last thing I do." That's the breakup of many friendships, the dissolving of many business partnerships, and the road to divorce.

Sure, we get hurt! No, we don't like it! It enrages us because it is so unnecessary. So often we end up the victims of someone else's stupidity or thoughtlessness. What hurts worst is when it is caused by "the one you love."

It's not easy to deal with those kinds of hurt. Our old nature screams for retribution. Yet we know there's a better way: "Do not repay anyone evil for evil. Be careful to do what is right in the eyes of everybody" (Rom. 12:17).

It's funny how the one we are most likely to hit back at is our spouse. Maybe that's because we can usually do it without anyone seeing it. But repaying evil for evil only worsens the problem, and sets the stage for more hurts: "Do not be overcome by evil, but overcome evil with good" (Rom. 12:21).

If we give in to a spirit of vengeance, we've lost the game. We have now been overcome by evil. We're just as bad as the person who hurt us. Actually worse. We had the chance to hold back, but we deliberately struck out.

Our goal is to be winners. To put an end to the game of hurting one another. To overcome the evil.

There's only one way to do that—"overcome evil with good."

It really works. Jesus proved it. Despised, rejected! Yet at the very worst moment of pain and sorrow, as He hung transfixed to the cross, He did not damn those who cursed Him. Instead He prayed, "Father, forgive them; for they know not what they do."

That was a personal victory, but not His ultimate triumph. That came when His resurrection proved that His sacrifice to atone for the sin of all mankind was sufficient and complete. He had overcome all evil. And He did it for us.

It's not easy to follow His example. But it is the way to overcome.

PRAYER

*J*esus, King and Savior, as I see You on the throne of glory, I rejoice in how You overcame the shame and abuse You endured. I know Your way of overcoming evil with good is the only way. Help me to do it too. Help me find enough joy in seeing how easily my hurts heal that I'm not even tempted to repay evil with anything other than good. Amen.

THE ART
OF FORGIVING

P aul's important directive to all Christians is dou-
bly important in marriage:

"As God's chosen people, holy and dearly beloved
... bear with each other and forgive whatever grievances you may have against one another. Forgive as
the Lord forgave you" (Col. 3:12–13).

All expressions of love are great. But there is none
more Christlike than that of forgiving. And none more
difficult.

It is unfortunate that as Christians—even in the
close bond of love we enjoy in our marriage—there is
the need to forgive, and to be forgiven.

Despite our good intentions and sincere efforts, we
often err and offend. Ever since sin intruded into our
world, we are not perfect people.

That's hard to accept—much harder to accept in
others than in ourselves. We're often blind to our own
faults, while the faults of others are conspicuously before our eyes. And whose do we see more frequently
than those of our own spouse?

"Bear with each other." Be patient and understanding. Don't be too quick to critize and condemn.
"Forgive whatever grievances you may have against
one another."

Sure, we're disappointed. Yes, we have reason to
expect more of each other. But is love that fickle that
it self-destructs with each little irritation?

But when it happens over and over? Doesn't there
come a time when we protect ourselves from getting

hurt anymore? When we just refuse to take it anymore?

It's hard! We all know the feeling! And it isn't making it any easier when Jesus comes along and says: "If he sins against you seven times in a day, and seven times comes back to you and says, 'I repent,' forgive him" (Luke 17:4).

Jesus' disciples' response was "Lord, increase our faith!" Our reply might be more earthy, "Are You kidding?" Either is a confession that we could never manage such forgiveness on our own.

But it is possible to learn. It comes as we seek His power to follow His example. "Forgive as the Lord has forgiven you."

PRAYER

*E*ternal Father, when we think of all You have forgiven us, and the price that Jesus paid for our eternal pardon, we see no other option when others wrong us. Increase our faith, that we may learn to forgive as we have been forgiven. Amen.

SEEKING FORGIVENESS

*T*here is another aspect to this whole matter of forgiving and forgetting. The Christian is not expected to go though life simplistically repeating, "You're forgiven—you're forgiven—you're forgiven" every time something goes wrong.

That is brought out well in these words of Jesus (Luke 17:4): "If he sins against you seven times in a day, and seven times comes back to you and says, 'I repent,' forgive him."

A willingness to forgive even repeated offenses is expected of a Christian. But so is a readiness on the part of the offender to come and say and honestly mean, "I repent!"

What does it mean if you say, "I forgive you!" to a person who doesn't care whether or not he has done wrong, or whether or not he is forgiven?

Such attitudes will wreak havoc in any relationship. How can anyone say, "I'm sorry!" and then go right out and do the same hurtful things all over again? We become callous to the doleful look and the whining apology which seem little more than a ploy to avoid being hurt in return.

Good marital ties require honest caring for one another. Two people truly close need to do a lot of forgiving. But that is only possible when we sincerely repent of each hurt inflicted, and sincerely desire to be forgiven.

We can't close our eyes and walk away from the wrongs we do, hoping they won't be noticed or felt. Nor can we hope the other will just graciously overlook them. That would belittle a serious situation.

Marriages need frequent times of cleansing—recognizing and excising offensive malignant growths—then applying the touch of healing love. First the surgery, then the healing.

Otherwise, it's like a sick man hoping the doctor will not find what's wrong, so that he won't have to undergo treatment. The condition will only worsen, until it is all cleaned out.

As Christians we should be well aware of this. We have a God whose love is great enough to forgive anything. But He also expects repentance and an earnest desire to be forgiven.

It's no different in marriage!

PRAYER

*F*ather, we remember the woman who anointed Jesus' feet with costly perfumes. He praised her, noting that she had been forgiven much, and consequently she loved much. Give us joy in our forgiveness too, and fill us with appreciative love. Amen.

SHIFTING
THE BLAME

When things go wrong, we generally face two courses of action. One is to look at the situation squarely, and determine to what degree we were responsible. The other is to look around to find someone or something else to blame.

Unfortunately, the latter is the most comfortable. Consequently, that is the action that most of us take.

It was so almost at the beginning. The perfect tranquillity of the Eden God created for man was broken when Adam and Eve both disobeyed God. Yet when God asked why, neither one was honest enough to confess openly: "I'm sorry! I disobeyed! I have no excuse! All I can do is ask for Your merciful pardon!"

Instead, Adam's response to God's *Why?* was "The woman you put here with me—she gave me . . . and I ate."

Eve's response was no better:

"The serpent deceived me, and I ate" (Gen. 3:12–13).

Eve blamed the tempter. Adam blamed Eve. And when it came right down to it, he even tried to shift some of the blame to God Himself, insinuating that he might never have sinned if God had not complicated his life by giving him a wife.

We shake our heads at their naive attempt to absolve themselves. But have we advanced in the art of accepting blame? Because we live in a complex society, it is easy to put the finger on others when something goes wrong. At work, where so many others are involved, we can easily get away with excusing ourselves without even pointing an accusing finger at anyone else. We just blame the system.

But it's not that easy at home, where only two shoulder the full responsibility. Yet it still happens, even there.

At the slightest provocation we indulge ourselves in thinking it was the other person's fault. Each such conclusion, expressed or unexpressed, is a wedge that pries the two of us apart.

Why do we let it? What difference does it make whose fault it was? True, we need to identify the trouble spots, and to face up to how each of us contributed to the problem. Only then can we begin to work together to overcome them.

That takes courage—the willingness to see ourselves as others see us—and as God sees us. That's when the problem ends, and the solution begins.

PRAYER

A lmighty God, give us the insight to see ourselves as we are, the vision to see what You would have us be, and the power and courage to become what You want us to be. In Jesus' precious name we ask it. Amen.

GREAT EXPECTATIONS

*I*t is disturbing to sense that we are not living up to expectations. We need to ask ourselves right then why we feel that way.

Sometimes we make unreasonable demands on ourselves. Martha got caught up in that syndrome when she entertained Jesus (Luke 10:38–42). She wanted everything to be just right for her honored guest. She flitted about from one thing to the next, "distracted by all the preparations," getting more "upset" all the time. Finally, she exploded at her sister, who pretty much left her to do it all alone.

Jesus reprimanded Martha gently. He did not come to be fussed over. He'd have preferred her company—to leave the dishes and just sit with Him and listen to His Word.

Sometimes, like Martha, we are uptight only because we demand more of ourselves than we properly should. We are so intent on doing things *for* each other, that we do not have much time to do things *with* each other.

There are also those many times when we let ourselves become the victims of the expectations of others. The harder we try to comply, the more the demands multiply. Everybody knows that "they can count on us."

Why? We never agreed. We were never even consulted. We were just suddenly told what we should be doing. Our relatives lay it on us. The demands at work are exhausting. Civic pride and good citizenship make claims on us. Our friends keep pulling us in all directions. Even our church persists in getting us more involved in congregational activities.

Sure, there's worth in all of the above. But we have needs too. So who has the responsibility of calling the shots? Isn't it we?

We are responsible for setting the priorities in our life. We together must determine what is most important—what will bring the greatest blessings, to ourselves and to others. We must learn to say "No" as well as "Yes," and to do it without apology or sense of guilt. We must establish our own agenda of requirements and expectations.

Micah 6:8 should be a lot of help to us in this: "What does the Lord require of you? To act justly and to love mercy and to walk humbly with your God."

In God's perspective the expectations for our lives can and should be pretty fundamental. Lord, show us how to take it from there!

PRAYER

A lmighty God, we don't want to shirk responsibility. Jesus didn't. But we don't want to bear unnecessary burdens. Neither did He. Make our expectations more in line with Your requirements, that our time and activities may become more properly balanced, and more indicative of our love and faith. Amen.

"GIVE US THIS DAY!"

"Teach us to number our days aright, that we may gain a heart of wisdom." Ps. 90:12

This entire prayer-poem of Moses reminds that time is a precious gift of God. Though God is eternal, we are not. Our life here and now has definite limitations.

There are just so many years, just so many days. God help us to make the most of them! That's the gist of Moses' prayer. Lord, keep us conscious that time is rapidly passing, and make us wise enough to make every day count.

"Give us this day," Lord. Not just our daily bread. The day itself, Lord, and all the joys and blessings and special opportunities it offers,

What have we been putting off? What are the "musts" that we have reserved for "some day" in the future? They must be important, or we would not keep thinking about them and planning around them.

Well, God has given us *this* day—just for things like that!

It is here now! That nebulous "some day" may never arrive. Must we not take at least that first step now, and *do* instead of delay?

Today should be just the right day for that long-intended helping hand, that extra act or word of love that can bring significant change.

Today should be just the right day for completely turning over our hearts and lives to God, to begin that closer walk in the better direction.

Today is the right day to summon up the courage to say "No!" to those pressures that have been rubbing away at our integrity and faith, and at the sanctity of our home and marriage.

Today is the right day to recommit ourselves to our God, and to each other.

If we can't or won't do it today, by what stretch of the imagination do we think we can do it tomorrow? Or ever?

PRAYER

*E*ternal Father, thank You for this day. It may be but a speck of eternity. But it is our moment of opportunity right now. Make us take the time—today—to recognize our failings and omissions. But not to discuss plans to do something about them "some day." Today, Lord! Make this a new beginning . . . the dawn of new hope . . . renewed faith anchored in Your eternal Word of promise. Today, Lord, make us totally alive in You! Through Jesus our Savior. Amen.

THE UPPER HAND

S o much of life is a jockeying for position. A striving to get and keep the upper hand.

We feel most comfortable when we are in charge. We like to set the pace; we like to establish the course. Let others do the adjusting.

It is not unusual then when we carry that pattern over into our married life, too.

Isn't that implied even in Scripture? It describes the husband as "the head of the wife" (Eph. 5:23) and states that "wives should submit themselves to their husbands" (v. 24).

It does indeed describe fitting relationships and responsibilities. But it is not talking about getting the upper hand.

The stage-setting principle is clearly set in verse 21: "Submit to one another out of reverence for Christ." If we honor and respect our Lord Jesus Christ, or attitude will show itself in our personal and private lives, and also in our relationships and dealings with others.

As fellow Christians we are to strengthen and encourage one another (19) and together "always [give] thanks to God the Father for everything in the name of our Lord Jesus Christ" (20).

In marriage that goes double. We don't strive to get our way, either by lording it over the other, or by whining and complaining. We are not living for self. We're living for each other.

That's really an extended application of our relationship with Christ. Follow it through in 2 Cor. 5:15:

"He died for all [*He submitted to and for us*], that those who live should no longer live for themselves but for him who died for them and was raised again."

We now submit to and for Him.

No more perfect pattern for marriage is possible. There are no higher motives, no greater blessings.

"Honor Christ by submitting to each other" (Eph. 5:21 TLB).

PRAYER

*L*ord Jesus Christ, fill our hearts with such love for each other that we may be more inclined to submit to each other rather than rule over the other . . . to give to each other rather than ask of the other. Keep us mindful that this is the path You first walked for us, the path on which You lead us to eternal blessing. Amen.

HEADING UPSTREAM

*E*arly in school we learned about the salmon who swim upstream to spawn. Each year the salmon return to the very stream in which they were hatched. There they lay their eggs to assure a new generation.

Though it's interesting to read about, it's exciting to actually see salmon fighting against the swift current. They rest in quiet pools to gain enough strength. Then they dash and leap to hurdle rocks and white water. Some are dashed back onto shallow rocks and shelves. Red flesh shows through jagged cuts in their skin. But they flounder and flip back into deeper, quieter water and rest again for another try.

They persist, to reach their ultimate goal. And a new life cycle begins.

One thing comes through. It's really hard to progress upstream, even to stay where you are, when a flood-stage current is sweeping almost everything the other way.

That's one of the challenges we face in marriage. It's not easy to make a good marriage, and hold home and family together in the context of today's society.

Why are so many marriages washing out? Basically because so many are content to go with the stream. The media that shape people's opinions—television, movies, newspapers, magazines, modern music and art—are increasingly depicting infidelity, sex outside marriage, divorce, homosexuality as being acceptable. The runoff from that watershed has reached flood proportions. And all too many are willing to "go with the flow."

"Do not conform any longer to the pattern of this world," Rom. 12:12 warns us. "But be transformed by the renewing of your mind. Then you will be able to test and approve what God's will is—his good, pleasing and perfect will."

Accept and conform to popular standards, and we may find ourselves drifting along with a lot of marriages that are being washed away.

But we want a marriage that grows stronger daily. That's what God wants for us, too.

Then it's time to reset our sights, renew our commitment, and make sure we are on course. It's an upstream persistence—going against the flow. It requires transformation, a complete change from the trends around us. Upward and onward!

PRAYER

*L*ord, give us the faith, courage, and stamina to go against the stream. Give us the joy of knowing that when we are going Your way we are going the right way, and that we have each other and You to encourage and help us all the way. Amen.

IN SICKNESS AND HEALTH

The Chamber of Commerce in one wet and foggy Pacific community boasts: "If you don't like our weather, wait a few minutes. It will change."

Everything changes. But constant change can be unsettling. It makes us feel insecure. We'd like to hold on to a few yesterdays when we finally had everything in place. We'd like to avoid a few tomorrows as we see a buildup of threatening storm clouds.

But we are not always in control. Sometimes we must just accept and adjust. How good are we at that?

God spare us the trials Old Testament Job experienced! But God give us a resolute faith like his when trials and problems do confront us! "The Lord gave and the Lord has taken away; may the name of the Lord be praised" (Job 1:21).

It's pretty hard to say and mean "The Lord be praised" when disaster strikes and you lose your children and your business and most of your life savings, as Job did.

We are more prone to pity ourselves and struggle with God. "Why, Lord?" We try to pinpoint whose fault it is, and we tend to turn on one another.

Yet when we spoke our marital vows to each other, we were aware that the high of those exciting days would not last forever. The honeymoon would be over. There would be cloudy, stormy days.

We even acknowledged that in the words of promise we spoke: "I take you . . . for better or for worse, for richer or poorer, in sickness and in health."

Of course, it's easy to talk big when everything is fine. But the real test comes in living out those intentions—in sticking to them when some of our world seems to be falling apart.

Isn't that when we need to hold onto each other all the more? And take a tighter grip on God's hand? God will not forsake us. He offers renewed hope and strength. He can bring us safely through all difficulties. "The Lord be praised!"

"I am convinced that [nothing] will be able to separate us from the love of God that is in Christ Jesus our Lord" (Rom. 8:38–39).

Or from each other!

PRAYER

*F*ather, we're not asking You to insulate us from trials and problems. Rather, help us struggle through them so that our marriage becomes stronger, and our trust in You deeper. We ask this in the name of Jesus, whom You sent to help us. Amen.

QUIET
TIME

As important as it is for us to communicate with each other, and with God, we also need our quiet time. A time to think alone—to sort out the pieces and reassemble them—to evaluate and regroup.

We need to get away from our daily schedule—the demands of others—the noise and confusion that surrounds us.

Vacations are good for this unless we structure them as inflexibly as we do the rest of the year. But we don't have to wait 50 weeks to find some quiet time. There are many moments in the day, and many more at night, that lend themselves well to reflection and meditation.

There have been nights when we've felt like David: "I am worn out from groaning; all night long I flood my bed with weeping and drench my couch with tears" (Ps. 6:6).

More than once we've decided that we're not going to bed. We are not going to struggle through another night tossing and turning. We would rather lose the sleep and keep our minds actively engaged on other things.

Thank God, we can generally use our quiet hours more productively than in the shedding of tears. So could David, "On my bed I remember you; I think of you through the watches of the night. Because you are my help, I sing in the shadow of your wings. My soul clings to you; your right hand upholds me" (Ps. 63:6–8).

Such quiet hours in the night can have a positive

effect on our faith and on our life. It's almost like attaching a trickle charger to our battery. We tap into our loving God as we lie there communing quietly with Him, and draw new power and purpose from Him. It happens so quietly and imperceptibly. But it does happen.

Best of all, it's more than casual contact. Our reaching to God is directly related to those matters that concern us. As David counseled, "When you are on your beds, search your hearts and be silent. [Then] offer right sacrifices and trust in the Lord" (Ps. 4:4–5).

What a marvelous opportunity to put our time to good use and then to rise in the morning and give joyous thanks to God for the new spirit He has put in us.

PRAYER

Dear Lord, with all the blessings You lavish on us daily, give us also moments of quiet time. Help us to use this time profitably, by giving You the opportunity to adjust our thoughts to Your will. Guide us by Your Spirit, that Jesus may become more fully the center of our lives. Amen.

TIME TO RETREAT?

M y, how the pressures of life can close in! We give our best all day long at work, and come home exhausted. We are greeted with other demands. We turn on our television set to get a little relaxing diversion, and all of today's problems in our community, nation, and world get dumped on us.

> Oh, that I had the wings of a dove! I would fly away and be at rest—I would flee far away and stay in the desert; I would hurry to my place of shelter, far from the tempest and storm.
>
> Psalm 55: 6–8

Who has been reading our mind? You mean that people way back then—in the good old days when life was slower and less complicated—got to feeling that way too?

Obviously! Modern man, living in the fast lane of today's technological society, has not cornered the market on tension and frustration. The context is different, but little else is.

Did they manage to escape, while we can not? Where did they find strength to face another day?

The answer does not lie in running and hiding. Our pressures and problems will not disappear because we close our eyes to them. Others of God's children found that, though a time of retreat is necessary and beneficial, the solution lies in seeking and finding new strength to advance and conquer.

> Those who hope in the Lord will renew their strength. They will soar on wings like eagles; they will run and not grow weary, they will walk and not be faint.
>
> Is. 40:31

The time of exhaustion may well be a time to retreat. But not in the sense of quitting or running away. Rather, it is a time to run to God, and find strength and refuge in Him. A time to let Him recharge our spirit, to renew our faith.

Then we can run and soar again, and walk without fainting. That's the joy of the Christian who is not afraid of being overwhelmed—who knows that by the grace and power of his loving God he can and will overcome all that life can throw at him.

PRAYER

G od is our refuge and strength, an ever -present help in trouble. Therefore we will not fear, though the earth give way and the mountains fall into the heart of the sea.

Ps. 46:1–2

Even though I walk through the valley of the shadow of death, I will fear no evil, for You are with me.

Ps. 23:4

HARMONY

*I*n marriage as in music there's much to be said for harmony. It makes for a smoother, more beautiful and enjoyable life together.

Not that we can't take discord. We've actually grown quite accustomed to the loud, clashing discord of many modern compositions. We might even enjoy it to a degree, working though it like a complex mathematical problem, breathing a sigh of relief when it all comes out all right.

But our nerves stretch only so far. Then we look for concord to replace discord, and harmony to dispel the building tensions.

Perfect harmony is not easy to achieve, even between two people very much in love with each other. We've not been stamped out of the same mold. We have differing backgrounds and experiences. Our tastes and emotions and interests are not identical. It's inevitable that there are and ever will be times when we do not fully see eye to eye.

How then can we settle our differences without quarrels and arguments? How can we disagree without becoming disagreeable?

It may be difficult, because our ideas and feelings are very personal. They reveal what we hold dear. Attack them, and you threaten us. As Solomon said in Proverbs 18:19: "Disputes are like the barred gates of a citadel." Apply force, and you only provoke more resistance. You need an open hand, not a clenched fist, to remove the barrier.

Obviously, Solomon had trouble applying these principles to his own life. Desexing several of his proverbs, we read: "Better to live on a corner of the roof than share a house with a quarrelsome [spouse]" (Prov. 21:9).

"A quarrelsome [spouse] is like a constant dripping on a rainy day; restraining her [or him] is like restraining the wind or grasping oil with the hand" (27:15–16).

No explanations are needed.

You can't win over a spouse—or anyone else—to your point of view with bulldozer tactics. Agreement is reached not as much by forcefulness as by a loving meeting of the minds.

Nor can you convert a person to a living faith by arguing. Arguments soon become the "constant dripping on a rainy day." Warm invitations and prayers will help. But it takes the gentle stirring of the Spirit through the Word of God to bring about the real change.

PRAYER

*H*eavenly Father, bless our marriage with harmony. Though we differ, like strings and brass in an orchestra, blend us into one beautiful orchestration. Weave our individualities into one harmonious counterpoint. Make us wholly one. Amen.

PEACE!

A bumper sticker cynically states: "War is hell! So is peace!"

What disillusioned the writer? What problems caused such a jaundiced view of life?

It's true that war is hell. That is an apt description of its bloodshed and destruction. Yet if a person really believes in what he is fighting for, and devotes all his energies and will to that cause, he can make it through even that worst of times.

But peace? Hell? Strangely enough, if a person does not know or believe in what he is living for, even the time of peace can become a hell of its own. It can be a time of tension and conflict within, which may generate tensions and conflicts without.

That's what Jesus was implying when He spoke of a peace which the world does not or can not give. Progress, prosperity, position, wealth really do not promise or provide peace. You'd think they would, since they are in line with most people's hearts' desires. But some of the greatest achievers in each of these areas admittedly ranked high in personal unhappiness and unrest.

What then is the key to true peace? Think through these words: "The Lord gives strength to his people; the Lord blesses his people with peace" (Ps. 29:11).

"You will keep in perfect peace him whose mind is steadfast, because he trusts in you" (Is. 26:3).

Real peace comes only from God Himself. It is something He promises and gives to His people.

God never promised us a world or life free from trials or problems, unhappiness or frustrations. Not even in the personal or family life of the Christian.

But He did make it possible for us to be anchored firmly, our hearts fixed and stayed by faith. When each storm subsides, we see again that we have not been moved. Shaken, but not moved. Because God has once again given us the strength to weather it all.

Peace lies in that confidence that through God we ever shall prevail—in our marriage too.

PRAYER

Almighty God, as pressures and problems assail us, make us wise enough to take a tighter hold on You. Do not let our hearts be troubled, neither let us be afraid. Calm our tense nerves with Your gentle yet powerful "Peace! Be still!" Because even the elements of storm and history respond to Your Word, we can live and sleep in peace in our unsettling world. Thank You, Father! We ask it in the name of Jesus. Amen.

OF MINDS
AND TONGUES

*T*wo of the great wonders of the human body are the mind and the tongue. They both stagger the imagination.

God blessed us with a mind that outstrips even the computer in its complexity and capability. He has given us almost unlimited potential to think, recall, reason, plan, and dream.

The tongue is equally marvelous. Bible translators, and others who get deeply involved in the study of linguistics, develop an awesome appreciation of that organ.

The tongue is a muscle, affixed predominantly on one end. Yet it is flexible and versatile enough to produce hundreds of sounds—and to do it precisely enough to result in intelligible languages—actually more than 5,000 recognizably different languages in today's world.

The tongue is a tool used by the mind to express complex and intricate concepts. Because of the combination of mind and tongue we have enjoyed an explosion of knowledge in the world these past years.

But what a responsibility this places on us. Scripture laments: "With the tongue we praise our Lord and Father, and with it we curse men, who have been made in God's likeness. Out of the same mouth come praise and cursing. My brothers, this should not be" (James 3:9–10).

James reminds how powerful the tongue is. He compares it to a bit in a horse's mouth, by which the rider can control and turn the whole animal (3:3)—to a ship's rudder, which is small but determines the course of the ship (3:4)—and to a spark that can set a whole forest ablaze (3:5).

With our minds and tongues we can build, or we can destroy. With them we can enourage, or we can crush. We can endear, or we can embitter.

We are aware of that, and we try to use our minds and tongues responsibly. But we are still quite careless in avoiding unintended hurts.

We have coined nice phrases to cover up such misuse. We speak of "thoughtlessness," "a slip of the lip," "it didn't come out quite right." Intended or not, we are still responsible. "You maybe didn't mean it, but deep down inside you were thinking it."

Where thoughtless words hurt most is in marriage. A stranger can easily shrug it off. But the one you love most?

PRAYER

*L*ord, fill our minds with loving thoughts and attitudes, so that we will use our tongues as tools, not weapons. Use them both to strengthen our bonds of love. In Christ. Amen.

WHERE DOES IT GO?

W e often get discouraged when we reconcile our monthly bank statements.

We work hard, but never seem to get ahead. We earn more than ever before, but never seem to have quite enough.

There's nothing new in that. It's not a sign of our times. For it really has more to do with personal attitudes than economics.

Listen to these words that sound contemporary, but which actually date back to the days when the Persian Empire was the greatest power on earth—about 500 years before the birth of Christ:

> The Lord Almighty says: "Give careful thought to your ways. You have planted much, but have harvested little. You eat, but never have enough. You drink, but never have your fill. You put on clothes, but are not warm. You earn wages, only to put them in a purse with holes in it. . . . You expected much, but see, it turned out to be little. What you brought home, I blew away."
>
> Hag. 1:5–6, 9

Why? Because they had their priorities mixed up. Maybe they truly were not making enough money. But the bigger problem was that they were spending it on the wrong things.

Their plan of money management—if they had one—was totally selfish and short-sighted. They were not "honoring the Lord with their wealth" (Prov. 3:9). They were conveniently forgetting that God is the Author and Giver of all good.

They scraped enough together to decorate the walls of their homes with beautiful and costly wood paneling. But they had nothing to spare for the Lord!

All right then, the Lord said. You say you can't afford to honor Me with your firstfruits. Let's see how well you do without My gifts. So their lives became a comedy of earning wages and stuffing them in pockets with holes—working harder and harder and having less and less to show for it.

Money management can be a real challenge to faith. To manage well, we need a desire to honor God, and the common sense to evaluate what is truly important—and spend accordingly.

We also need faith to truly believe what our Lord promises, "Give, and it will be given to you. A good measure, pressed down, shaken together and running over, will be poured into your lap. For with the measure you use, it will be measured to you" (Luke 6:38).

That's His promise! Do we trust Him enough to try it?

PRAYER

Father, thank You for the generous way You provide for us. Make us good managers of Your gifts, that we not squander them selfishly and foolishly. Teach us to invest wisely, that our spending patterns reflect our love for You and others. Amen.

WORK

M ore conflicts are generated over work than almost anything else.

"There was a man all alone; he had neither son nor brother. There was no end to his toil, yet his eyes were not content with his wealth. "For whom am I toiling," he asked, "and why am I depriving myself of enjoyment?" This too is meaningless—a miserable business!" (Eccl. 4:8).

One person regards work as a necessary evil. Another's life would be totally devoid of meaning and purpose if he could not immerse himself in his work.

A junior executive works hard and conscientiously and is a real credit to the company. But he also makes it known that he is a husband and father, and that the company is not his first love. The senior executive, who is married to the company, resents his unwillingness to spend his evenings and weekends at the office. He consistently blocks the young man's efforts to advance.

Sounds familiar! Where's the problem? Certainly not in work. Even in the utopia of Eden man found joy and satisfaction in working the garden and taking care of it (Gen. 2:15). Work was not a chore. It was a pleasure.

In our imperfect world work has become a chore. Sweat, blisters, and anxieties accompany it. But that has not made it an evil. Nor does Ecclesiastes suggest it. Rather, that we ask ourselves, "Why am I doing what I'm doing?" What are we really working for?

To make money? Obviously, that's part of the reason. It's the means to provide the food, clothing, shelter, transportation, and recreation essential to our personal and family health.

To amass money? That's a different story. If wealth is a major goal, we might as well tell the man in Ecclesiastes to move over. It then can become "a miserable business." The more you get, the more you want. Again it's not the wealth. Many of God's people have been blessed with above average riches. It's the attitude!

Some have gained the world, but lost their soul. They never rose above the spiritual poverty level. Yet some have gained the world and found great blessing in it. In addition to enjoyment of their blessings, they now had a chance to be generous—to serve the Lord with the plenty He had given them.

So why are we doing what we are doing? If we hate our jobs, let's consider making a change. Maybe God has something else in mind for us. Let's not be afraid to explore—or to offer ourselves to God: "Here we are, Lord! Use us!" And if we enjoy our work, let's thank God for it, and really work to His glory!

PRAYER

L ord God, help us find fulfillment in our work. No matter what it is, make it a true ministry. And let it be done in accordance with Your will, and to Your glory. In Jesus, amen!

BEST FRIENDS

*H*ow fortunate we are when we have a good friend. Not the old gang or the new neighbors. Just someone to whom we can turn when we need help—to whom we can open our hearts without fear of betrayal—who really knows us and is sensitive to us.

"A man of many companions may come to ruin, but there is a friend who sticks closer than a brother" (Prov. 18:24).

David had his Jonathan. When his life was threatened by King Saul and he had to remain in hiding, he and Jonathan, Saul's son, managed to get together. Though Jonathan risked his neck in these secret rendezvous, he was willing to take that chance. For they were friends. In his hours of deepest need, David found strength and solace in his friend.

Jesus said that when a man and a woman become one in marriage, they leave their parents. They also leave their friends. But here again it is not a total separation, but a change in relationship.

We no longer need constant companions. We now have each other. But we still cherish our friends. The bond of trust and mutual caring matures. That special tie with those special few can survive long absence and great distance. It is still important.

However, there are two friendships that need to blossom and grow much more over the years. The first is our friendship with each other. As husband and wife we must become and remain our own best friends.

We chose each other, and made a lifelong commitment. Why? Because we saw in each other the one, of all others, with whom we would most like to spend our lives.

We're best friends when we seek each other's company most of all—when we enjoy doing things together—when we have no trouble in sharing everything, even our deepest thoughts and feelings with each other.

There's yet another best friend we should not short-change. That is our loving God and Savior. Jesus said: "I have called you friends, for everything that I learned from my Father I have made known to you" (John 15:15).

"This is how we know what love is: Jesus Christ laid down his life for us" (1 John 3:16).

How could we ever find a better friend? Who else understands us so completely? Who else is so willing to accept us and love us just as we are? Who else would give up as much as He did, when He sacrificed even His life to secure our eternal future?

We have the best of all friends possible. Lord, help us to be that kind of friend too!

PRAYER

A s Jesus is a Friend to me, make me a friend to others. Amen.

A TIME
TO LAUGH

"There is . . . a time to weep and a time to laugh, a time to mourn and a time to dance" (Eccl. 3:1, 4).

Heaven help those who live in a house that has time for neither!

Tears, be they of sorrow or of joy, are therapeutic. When the heart is heavy, it's not a time to conjure up the macho male image that a man does not show emotion, or to sing the old song, "Big Girls Don't Cry."

It's a time to express our feelings honestly and openly with each other, and deal with our shared grief. It's a time for understanding and compassion—a time to uphold and encourage—to help each other draw on the strength and comfort of God's Word.

And when the heart is light, we should not grouse about not having time for such foolishness.

Sure, the Bible warns against humor that is pocked with "obscenity, foolish talk or course joking, which are out of place" (Eph. 5:4). But it speaks positively about a sense of humor and a bright and happy spirit.

We all need "a time to laugh." Listen to these verses from Proverbs:

"A happy heart makes the face cheerful, but heartache crushes the spirit" (15:13).

"The cheerful heart has a continual feast" (15:15).

"A cheerful heart is good medicine, but a crushed spirit dries up the bones" (17:22).

Are there not also words of wisdom in the Bible expressed almost with a smile?

"As vinegar to the teeth and smoke to the eyes, so is a sluggard to those who send him" (10:26).

"Better a meal of vegetables where there is love than a fattened calf with hatred" (15:17).

The Psalms are also saturated with joy and thanksgiving. Our whole relationship with our loving God is one to make us want to cheer and sing. The setting of our Christian home—the sharing of our life and love—our daily joys and blessings—it's enough to make us want to laugh and dance and sing.

It was Luther (was it not?) who, when he saw his wife with a long, sad face, teased: "What's the matter? Did God die?"

Well, God did not die! And we are alive! And we have each other! And far more! So let's enjoy the goodness of the Lord. It is in truth "a time to laugh."

PRAYER

L ord, our times are in Your hands. Bring them all together that, in happy or sad days, we never lose sight of Your love or the lasting joys You made ours through Jesus. Amen.

KEEP
IN TOUCH!

R each out and touch someone!" This slogan has
been used extensively by a major communications
company to stress the importance of keeping in touch
with one another.

The point is well made. In friendship as in business
it is imperative to maintain close contact. The closer
the better. "A man finds joy in giving an apt reply—
and how good is a timely word." (Prov. 15:23).

Notes and memos aren't good enough. There are
times and places where such one-way contact must suf-
fice. But it can never take the place of face to face and
voice to voice togetherness.

Such constant communication is the key to togetherness in our home too, is it not? Being together—keeping our hearts and minds open to each other—sharing
our thoughts and feelings freely with each other—is
the key to avoiding misunderstandings and strengthening our ties.

Sometimes we really have to work at it. There are
times we just do not feel like talking. But that can be
just as irritating and nonproductive to all concerned as
getting a busy signal or no answer on the telephone.

Those times when we just don't feel like discussing
what's weighing heavily on us are critical. They require
skillful handling. But those are the very moments when
we need extra support and love.

That comes through beautifully in the many Bible
texts that encourage us to pray, such as "Call upon me
in the day of trouble; I will deliver you, and you will
honor me" (Ps. 50:15).

When things go wrong, how are we helped by sitting in lonely silence, brooding? When we are troubled and confused, how are we benefited by hanging up on those who care most about us?

The essence of a good relationship is closeness. God is our ever-present Friend and Helper. Open up, and let His love come in. As husband and wife, we are each other's best friend. We need to be totally open at all times, and let love take over.

There's joy in giving and receiving "an apt reply," "a timely word." Keep in touch!

PRAYER

L ord, there are times when it seems all lines are down. Make us see it's more probable that we're just not plugged in. Help us to keep an open circuit with You, and with our loved ones. Teach us to communicate freely, that we may always be one in heart and one in mind. In Jesus we ask it. Amen.

CPSIA information can be obtained at www.ICGtesting.com
Printed in the USA
LVOW08s0237170614

390286LV00001B/1/P